AN IMAGINATION LIBRARY SERIES

WORLD'S LARGEST
SNAKES

Asian Rock Pythons

by Valerie J. Weber

Gareth Stevens Publishing
A WORLD ALMANAC EDUCATION GROUP COMPANY

Please visit our web site at: www.garethstevens.com
For a free color catalog describing Gareth Stevens Publishing's
list of high-quality books and multimedia programs,
call 1-800-542-2595 (USA) or 1-800-387-3178 (Canada).
Gareth Stevens Publishing's fax: (414) 332-3567.

Library of Congress Cataloging-in-Publication Data available upon request
from publisher. Fax (414) 336-0157 for the attention of the Publishing
Records Department.

ISBN 0-8368-3655-3

First published in 2003 by
Gareth Stevens Publishing
A World Almanac Education Group Company
330 West Olive Street, Suite 100
Milwaukee, WI 53212 USA

Text: Valerie J. Weber
Cover design and page layout: Scott M. Krall
Series editor: Jim Mezzanotte
Picture Researcher: Diane Laska-Swanke

Photo credits: Cover, pp. 5, 7, 9, 21 © Joe McDonald/Visuals Unlimited; p. 11 © McDougal
Tiger Tops/Ardea London Ltd.; p. 13 © Milton H. Tierney Jr./Visuals Unlimited; p. 15
© E. A. Kuttapan/naturepl.com; p. 17 © Craig Pelke; p. 19 © John Cancalosi/naturepl.com

Printed in the United States of America

1 2 3 4 5 6 7 8 9 07 06 05 04 03

Front cover: Like all snakes, an Asian rock python can stick out its tongue without opening its mouth. Its tongue senses danger or dinner!

TABLE OF CONTENTS

Words that appear in the glossary are printed in **boldface** type the first time they occur in the text.

On Land or in Water

The Indian python and the Burmese python look a lot alike, and both of these big snakes are called Asian rock pythons. Some Asian rock pythons have grown to a length of 20 feet (6 meters), but most only grow to about 12 feet (3.7 m). Their bodies are very thick for their length. A 15-foot (4.6-m) python can grow as thick as a basketball!

Asian pythons can be found in the water and on land. They live in many different **habitats**, including river valleys, woodlands, rain forests, grasslands, swamps, marshes, and rocky foothills. The Asian python roams India, Myanmar (also known as Burma), and the island of Sri Lanka.

Four people are needed to display this Burmese python! Huge but gentle, Burmese pythons are easy to handle. They are often used in circuses.

Concealed by Color

A snake has overlapping **scales** that cover every part of its body. These scales often form beautiful designs, like patterns made with tiny tiles. The scales on an Asian rock python's back are smaller than the ones on its belly, and they make more complicated patterns.

The skin of an Asian rock python is tan-colored, with dark brown splotches that have black edges. Its head has a dark splotch in the shape of an arrow. The Asian python's light and dark brown colors match many of the colors that surround it. This **camouflage** helps the Asian python hide from both **predators** and **prey**.

This Asian rock python sparkles in the sun.
Many people think a snake's skin is slimy,
but it is actually smooth and dry.

A Surprise Attack

The Asian rock python is an **ambush** hunter. It lies on the ground or hangs in low tree branches, waiting for its prey to get close. This snake moves slowly, but when a victim is nearby, it strikes quickly!

The python has teeth that curve to the back of its mouth. These teeth help it hold tightly to its prey. With amazing speed, the Asian python wraps its **coils** around the animal. The snake squeezes until its prey has been **suffocated**.

Once the Asian python's prey is dead, the snake begins swallowing its meal. Tiny ripples appear on the python as it slowly pushes the food into its body.

The four different parts of the Asian rock python's jaw move separately from each other as the snake "walks" its mouth over a rat.

Prey for a Python

Asian pythons often live in forests, but they sometimes move into grasslands and **scrubland**. In any place that an Asian python lives, it will eat almost anything it can catch and fit into its body. When the python swallows its dinner, its mouth and throat both expand beyond their normal size.

Although the Asian rock python usually feeds on mammals such as Asian deer and wild pigs, it will also eat birds and other animals. The pythons have even been known to eat leopards!

This Asian rock python has captured a hog deer. After such a big meal, the python will not have to eat for a long time.

Goggles on a Snake?

If an Asian rock python is in the water, it is not trying to find a meal. Instead, the snake is soaking itself before it molts, or sheds its skin. The water also helps support the snake's heavy body, allowing it to rest. Asian pythons are good swimmers and can hold their breath underwater for up to thirty minutes. With an "S"-shaped motion, the Asian python swims through **tropical** streams and rivers.

A clear cap of skin protects the Asian python's eyes and keeps them from drying out. These caps are like goggles on a diver and help the snake see underwater. Like all snakes, the Asian rock python cannot close its eyes or blink. It actually sleeps with its eyes open!

12

When an Asian rock python sheds its skin, the snake also sheds the cap of clear skin that protects its eyes and helps it see underwater.

Is a Snake's Blood Really Cold?

Although snakes are **cold-blooded**, their blood is about the same temperature as **warm-blooded** creatures. They just keep their blood warm in a different way than warm-blooded animals.

Like all cold-blooded creatures, Asian pythons depend on the temperature outside their body to keep them warm. They move from warm sunlight to cool shade or water to adjust the temperature inside their bodies.

Giant snakes such as the Asian python take longer to warm up than smaller snakes. An Asian rock python cannot become active until its body temperature has risen to the right level. All giant snakes live in warm parts of the world.

This Asian rock python is soaking up the sun in India. The snake keeps its body heat just right to help it digest its food.

Keeping the Eggs Warm

A female Asian python can actually raise her body heat herself to warm her eggs. First, she gathers her eggs together into a pyramid-shaped mound. Then, the mother python coils her body around the eggs and rests her head on top of the pile, so she can protect them and control their temperature.

Finally, the mother python twitches, or shivers, to produce enough heat to warm her body and the eggs. She can raise the temperature inside the egg pile as much as 15° Fahrenheit (8° Celsius) above the temperature outside the pile.

Bigger female pythons produce a greater number of eggs. This large mother python is wrapped around seventy-two eggs!

Egg Problems

If a mother Asian python cannot keep her eggs warm enough, the baby snakes growing inside the eggs might have problems. If the eggs get too cold, the baby snakes inside will not grow.

Shivering takes a lot of energy from the mother python. She does not eat while she is protecting her eggs. Between the time she lays her eggs and the time they begin to hatch, she may lose up to half of her body weight. It may be two or three years before a mother Asian python gains enough weight and has enough energy to lay more eggs.

A baby python uses a special tooth called an egg tooth to break out of its leathery shell. The baby snake glides away, and the egg tooth soon falls off.

Threats to Asian Rock Pythons

Asian pythons face danger from natural enemies, such as crocodiles, leopards, and tigers. But people are the biggest threat to Asian rock pythons. The snakes are killed for their skin, which is used to make purses and belts, and for their blood, which is used in traditional medicines. The pythons are also killed for their meat. Live pythons are sold to zoos and to people who want them for pets.

The jungle habitats of Asian rock pythons are disappearing because people cut down trees for lumber and to make room for homes and farms. Today, however, India has set aside several large areas to protect the habitats of Indian pythons. It is also **illegal** to buy or sell an Indian python or any part of its body.

A Burmese python rests at water's edge. Burmese pythons are not in as much danger from people as Indian pythons, and they live well in zoos.

MORE TO READ AND VIEW

Books (Nonfiction)
Fangs! (series). Eric Ethan (Gareth Stevens)
Pythons. Animal Kingdom (series). Julie Murray (Abdo & Daughters)
Pythons. Animals & the Environment (series). Mary Ann McDonald
  (Capstone Press)
Pythons. Naturebooks (series). Don Patton (Child's World)
Pythons. Really Wild Life of Snakes (series). Doug Wechsler
  (Rosen Publishing Group)
Pythons. Snakes (series). James E. Gerholdt (Checkerboard Library)
Pythons and Boas: Squeezing Snakes. Gloria G. Schlaepfer and
  Mary Lou Samuelson (Franklin Watts, Inc.)
Snakes Are Hunters. Patricia Lauber (Bt Bound)

Books (Fiction)
How Snake Got His Hiss. Marguerite W. Davol (Orchard Books)
I Need a Snake. Lynne Jonell (Putnam Publishing Group)
Snake Camp. George Edward Stanley (Golden Books)

Videos (Nonfiction)
Amazing Animals Video: Scary Animals. (Dorling Kindersley)
Fascinating World of Snakes. (Tapeworm)
Predators of the Wild: Snake. (Warner Studios)
Snakes: The Ultimate Guide. (Discovery Home Video)

PLACES TO WRITE AND VISIT

Here are three places to contact for more information:

Black Hills Reptile Gardens
P.O. Box 620
Rapid City, SD 57709
USA
1-800-355-0275
www.reptile-gardens.com

Los Angeles Zoo
5333 Zoo Drive
Los Angeles, CA 90027
USA
1-323-644-6400
www.lazoo.org

Woodland Park Zoo
601 N. 59th Street
Seattle, WA 98103
USA
1-206-615-1017
www.zoo.org

WEB SITES

Web sites change frequently, but we believe the following web sites are going to last. You can also use good search engines, such as **Yahooligans!** [www.yahooligans.com] or **Google** [www.google.com], to find more information about Asian rock pythons. Here are some keywords to help you: *Asian rock pythons, Burmese pythons, Indian pythons, pythons, reptiles,* and *snakes.*

**www.amnh.org/nationalcenter/
Endangered/python/python.html**
An Indian python can lay sixty eggs at a time, but the wild population of Indian pythons is endangered. To find out why, visit *Indian Python*, a page from the web site of the American Museum of Natural History.

**www.bagheera.com/inthewild/
van_anim_python.htm**
Land that has been set aside for Indian pythons could provide firewood and food for people. At this page from the *Endangered* web site, you will find some good ideas for protecting the habitats of Indian pythons.

www.lazoo.org/baby.htm
How many people does it take to lift a 15-foot (4.6-m), 227-pound (103-kilogram) Indian python? Find out at *Baby the Indian Python,* from the Los Angeles Zoo's web site.

**www.schoolworld.asn.au/species/
python.html**
Indian Python is a web site created by two fourth-graders. They explain why hunters kill Indian pythons and what steps are being taken to protect these snakes.

**www.terravzw.org/english/
animal_on_the_spot/python_mol.htm**
Close-up photographs of a fully grown Burmese python and an Indian python make this site worth visiting. Find out which python has a darker color.

**www.zoo.org/educate/fact_sheets/
python/python.htm**
This *Animal Fact Sheets* page is from the Woodland Park Zoo's web site. Learn many interesting facts about the Indian python, including how the python kills its prey. You can also find out how to adopt a python!

GLOSSARY

You can find these words on the pages listed. Reading a word in a sentence helps you understand it even better.

ambush (AM-bush) — a surprise attack from a hidden place 8

camouflage (CAM-uh-flahj) — patterns and colors that make something look like part of its surroundings, so it is hard to see 6

coils (KOYLZ) — the circles a snake can form with its body 8

cold-blooded (kold BLUD-id) — having a body temperature that changes with the temperature of the air outside 14

habitats (HAB-uh-tatz) — places where an animal or plant lives and grows 4, 20

illegal (ih-LEE-guhl) — against the law 20

predators (PRED-uh-turz) — animals that hunt other animals for food 6

prey (PRAY) — animals that are hunted by other animals for food 6, 8, 10

scales (SKAYLZ) — small, stiff plates, made mostly of the same material as human hair and nails, that cover a snake's skin 6

scrubland (SKRUB-land) — an area of land that is covered with very short trees or bushes 10

suffocated (SUF-uh-kay-tid) — died from having no air to breathe 8

tropical (TROP-ih-cull) — being in a part of the world where the temperature is always warm and plants usually grow at all times of the year 12

warm-blooded (WARM blud-id) — having blood that stays at the same temperature, even when the air temperature outside the body changes 14

INDEX